Learn to Draw Cartoons : Pencil Drawings Step By Step

Pencil Drawing Ideas for Absolute Beginners

By GP Edu

Published By:

GP Edu

© Copyright 2015 – GP Edu

ISBN-13: 978-1507706091
ISBN-10: 150770609X

Table of Contents

How To
Draw
Doraemon

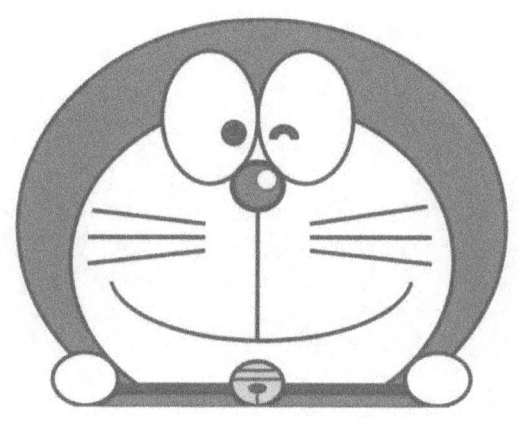

Step 1

Step 2

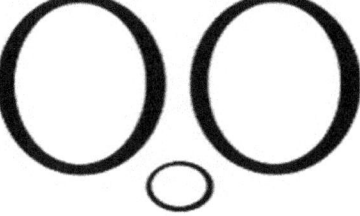

Step 3

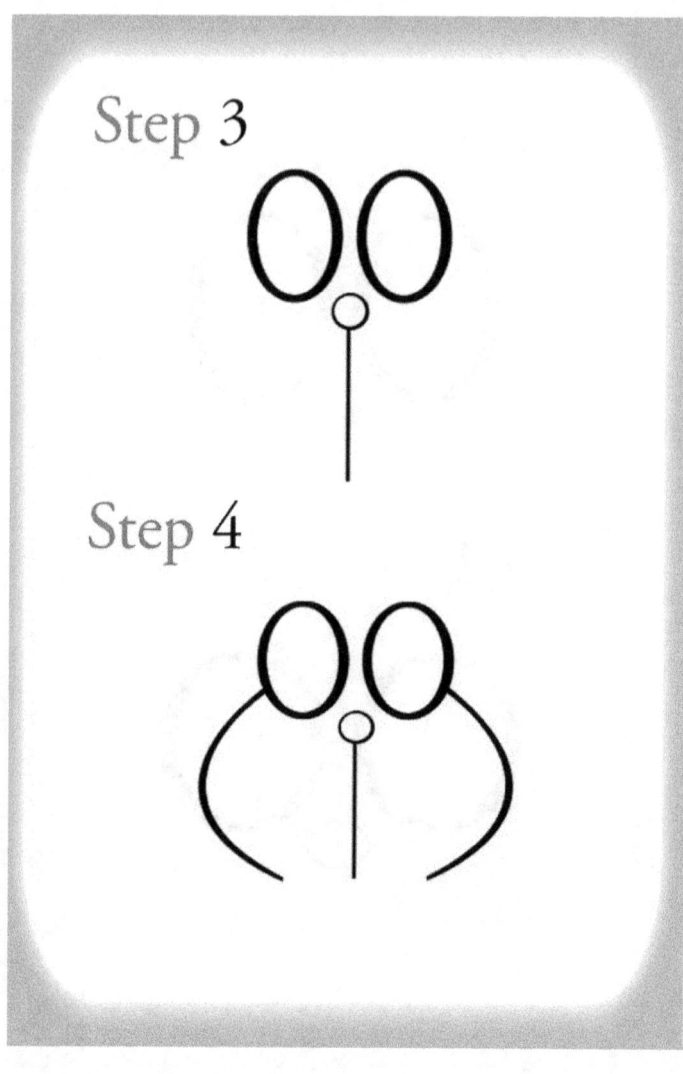

Step 4

Step 5

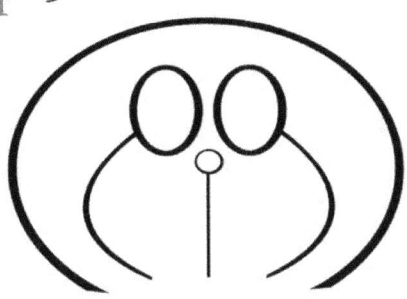

Step 6

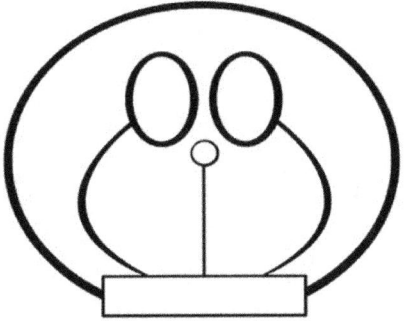

Step 7

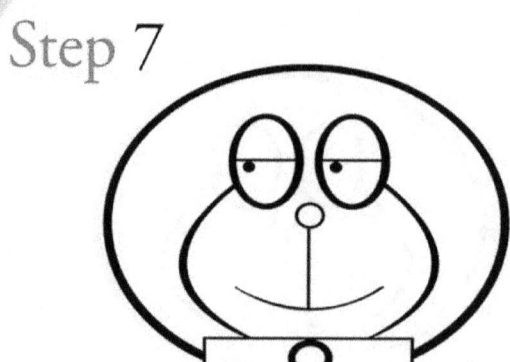

Step 8

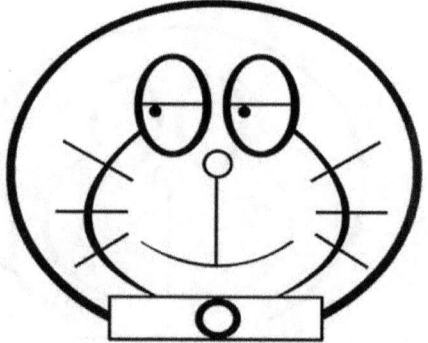

How To
Draw
Shrek

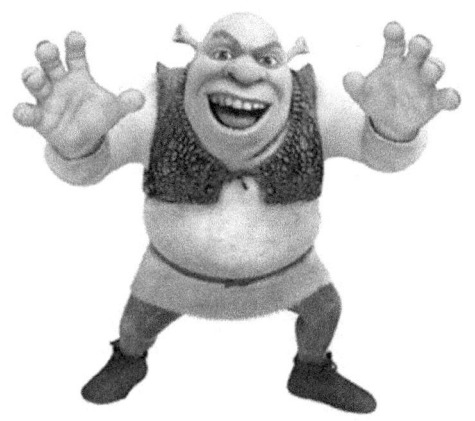

Step 1

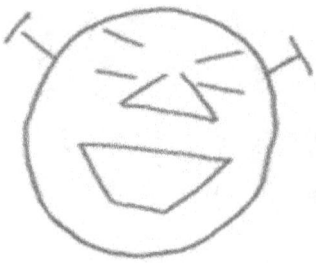

Step 2

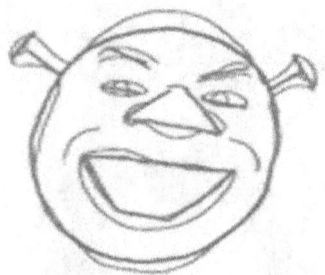

Step 3

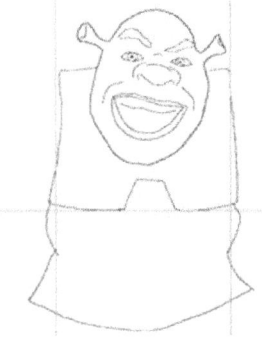

Step 4

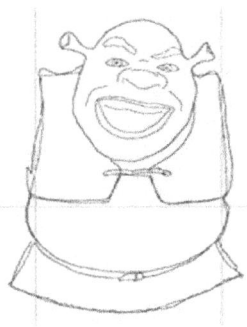

Step 5

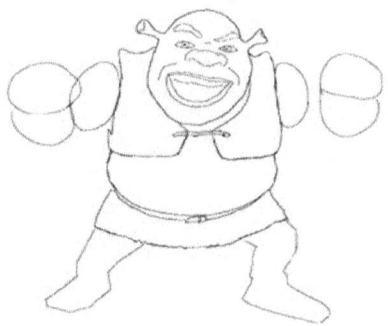

Step 6

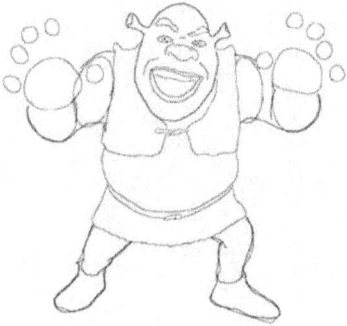

Step 7

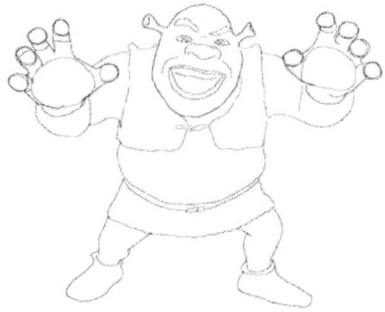

Step 8

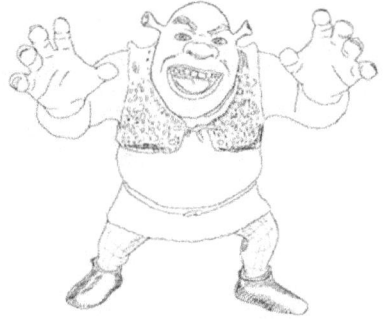

How To
Draw
Pingu

Step 1

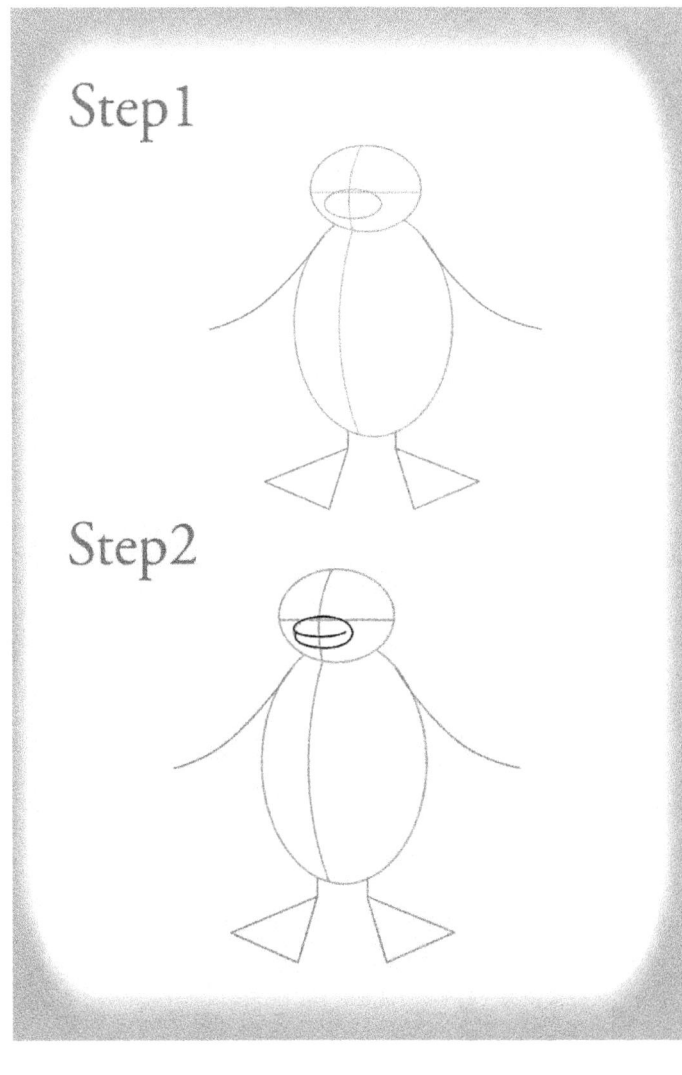

Step 2

Step3

Step4

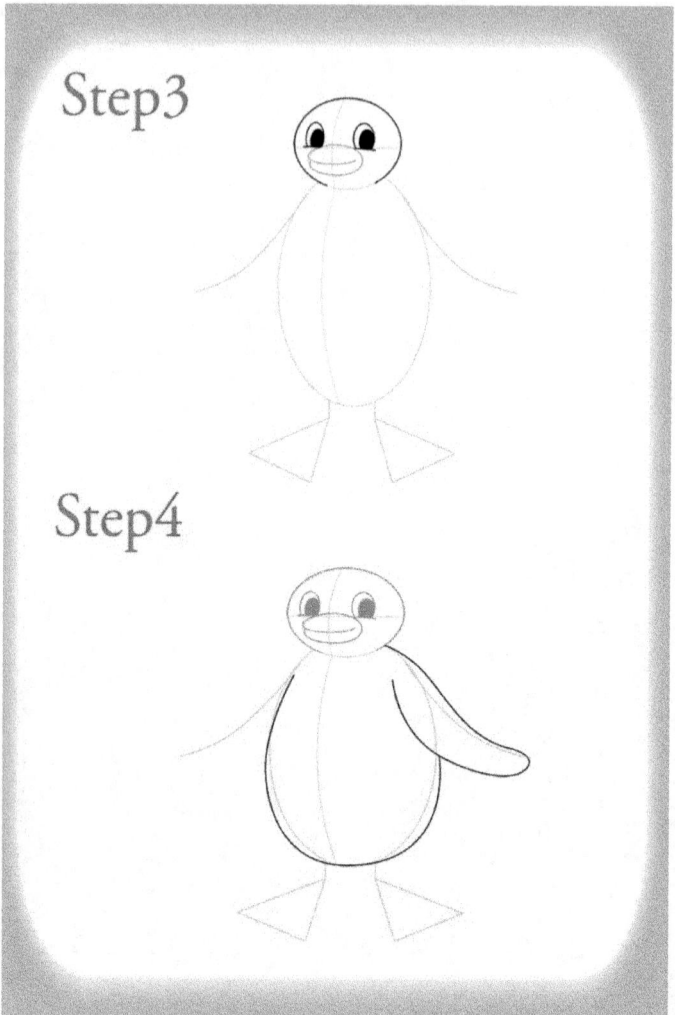

Step5

Step6

How
to
Draw Megaman

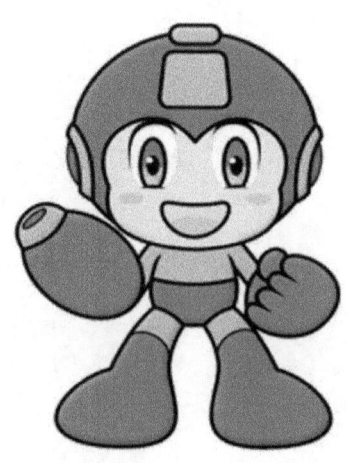

Step 1

Step 2

Step3

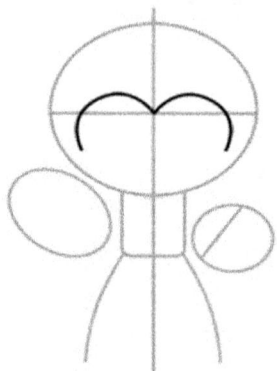

Step4

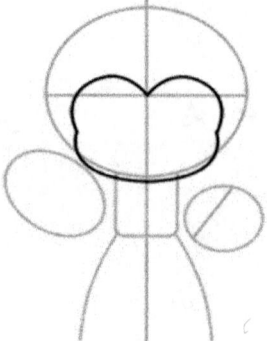

Step5

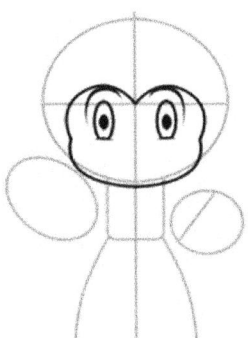

Step6

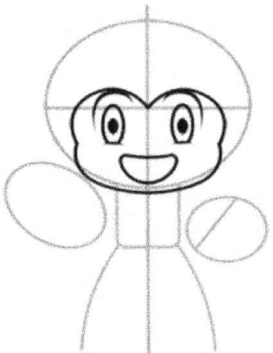

Step7

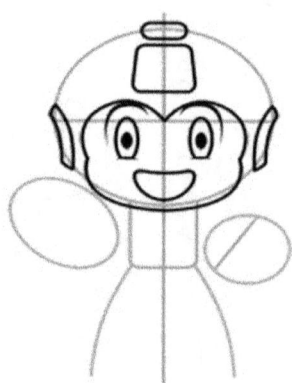

Step8

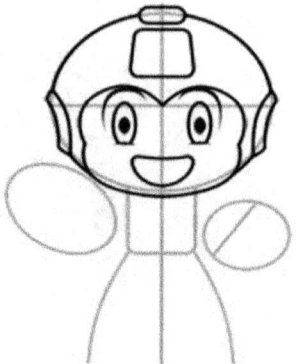

Step9

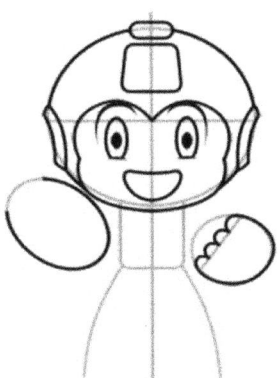

Step10

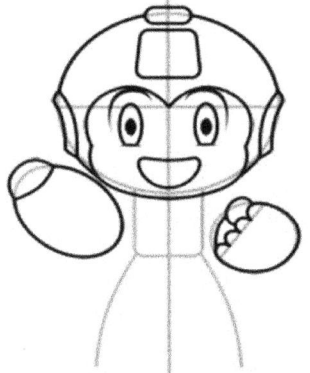

Step11

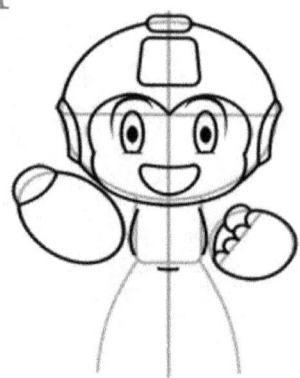

Step12

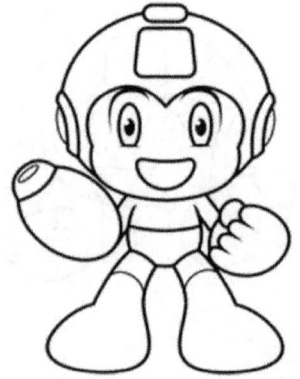

How to Draw Patrick Star

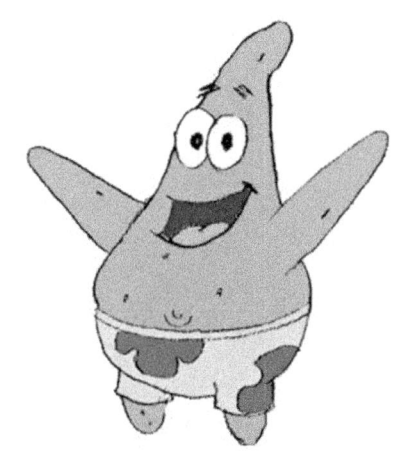

Step 1

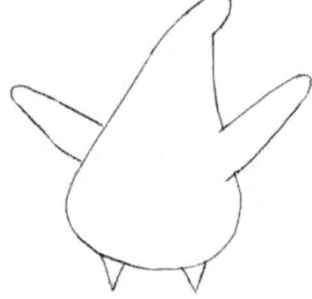

Step 2

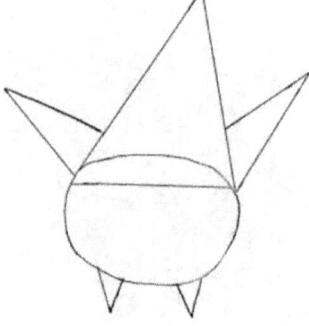

Step 3

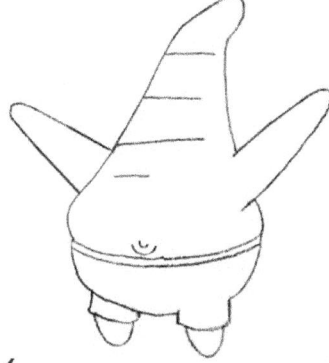

Step 4

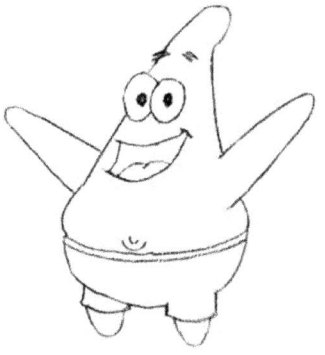

How To
Draw
Sonic Hedgehog

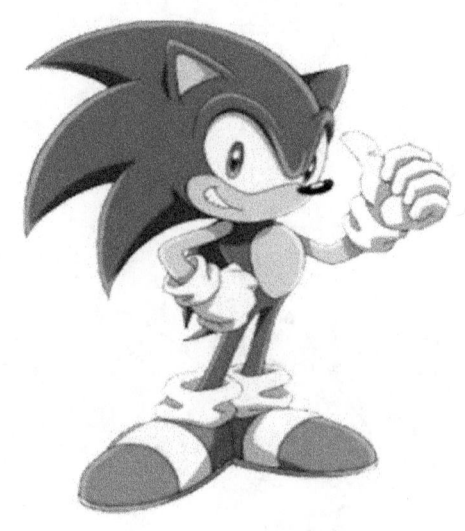

Step 1

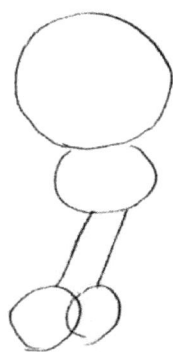

Step 2

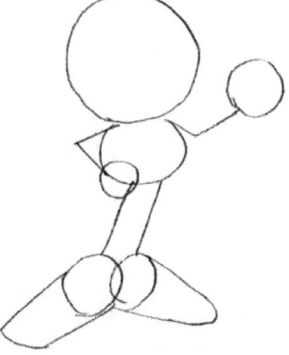

Step 3

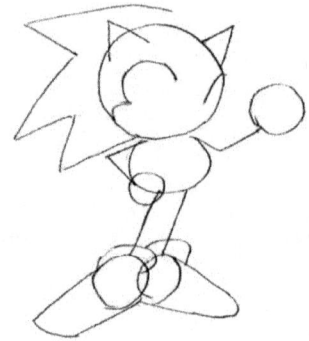

Step 4

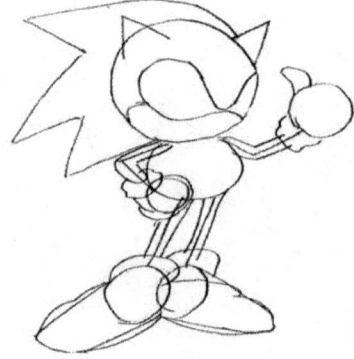

Step 5

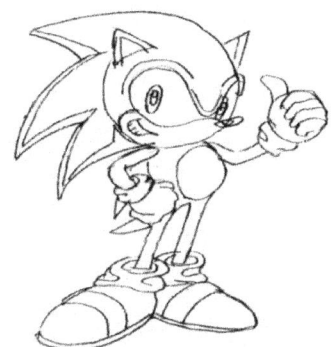

Step 6

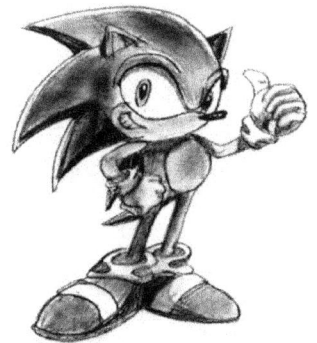

How To Draw
Spiderman

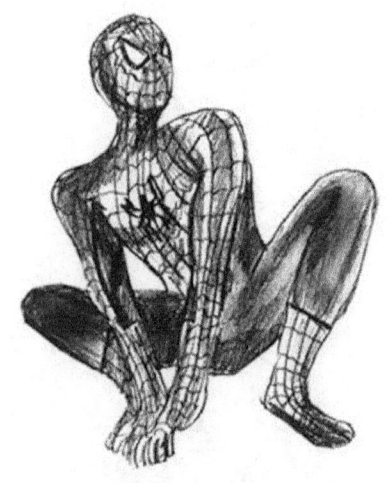

Step 1

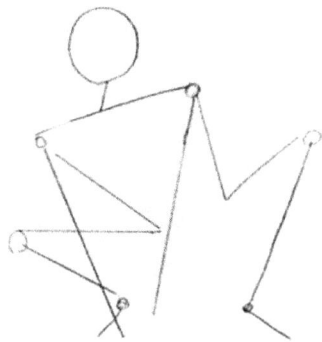

Step 2

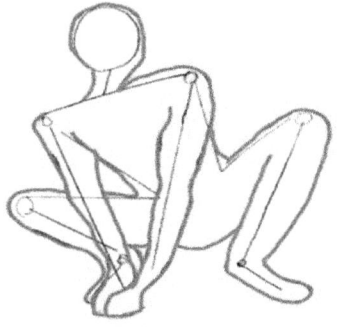

Step 3

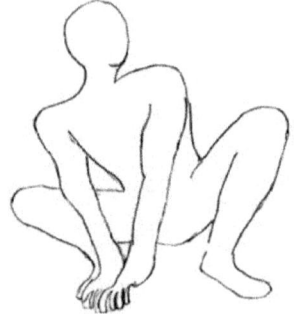

Step 4

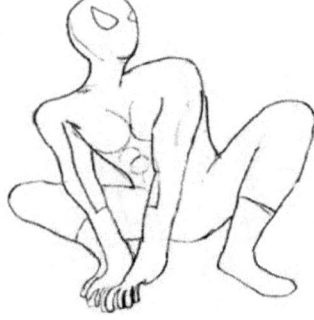

Step 5

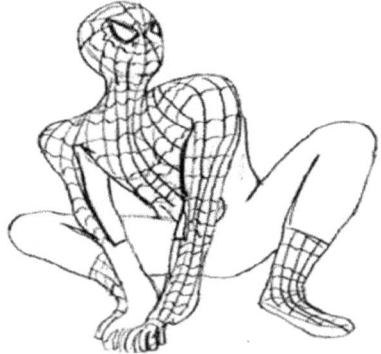

Step 6

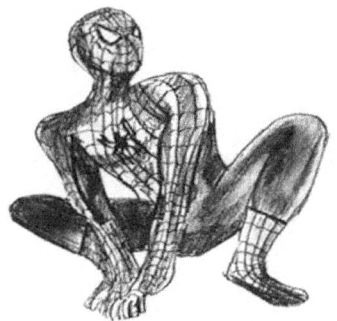

How To Draw
Pooh

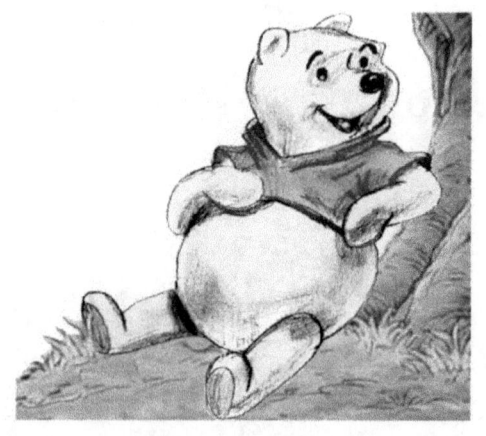

Step 1

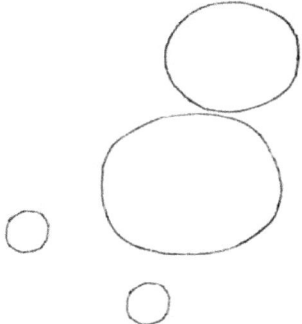

Step 2

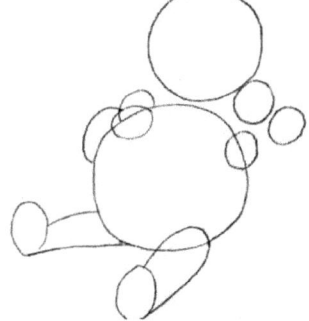

Step 3

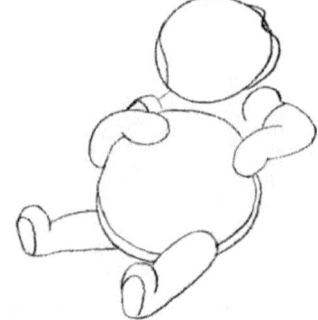

Step 4

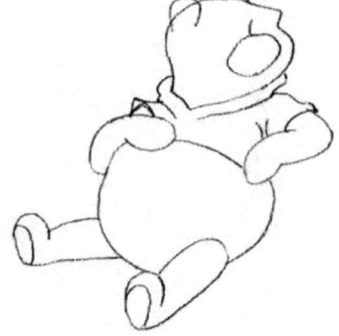

Step 5

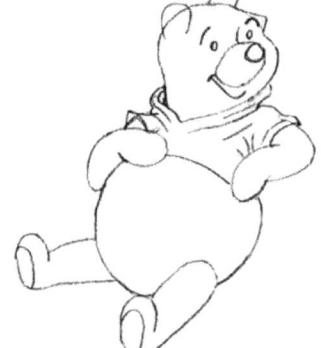

Step 6

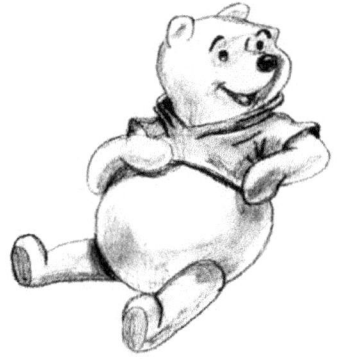

How To Draw
Winx Flora

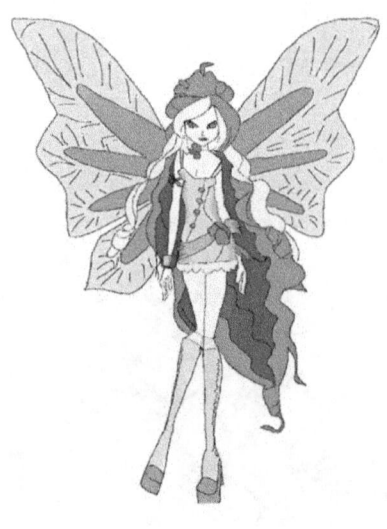

Step 1

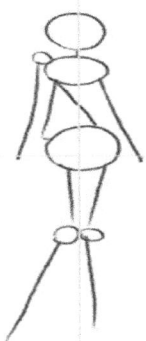

Step 2

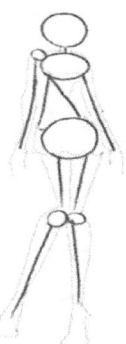

Step 3

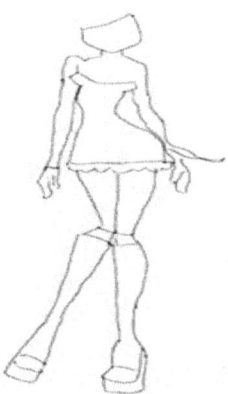

Step 4

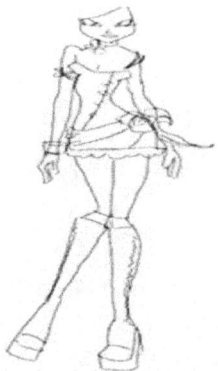

Step 5

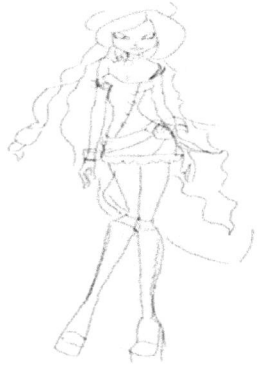

Step 6

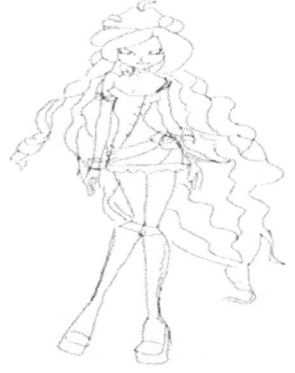

Step 7

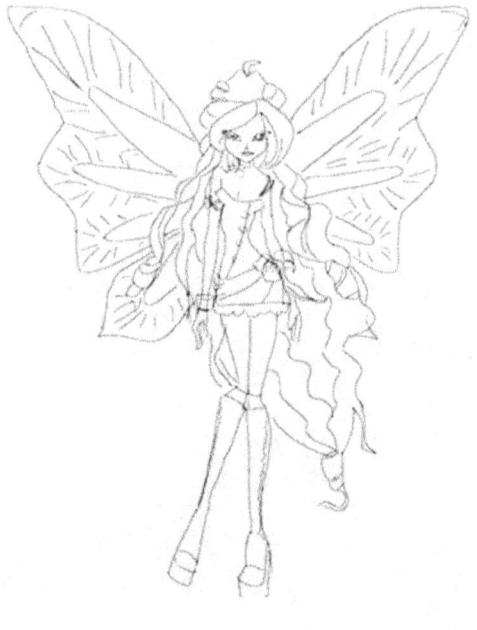

HOW TO DRAW PIKACHU

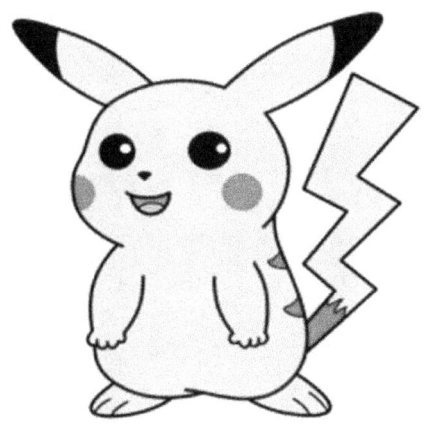

Step 1

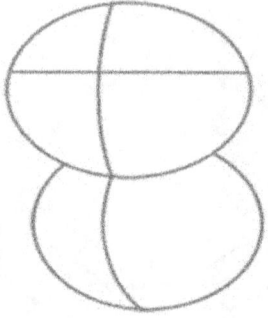

Step 2

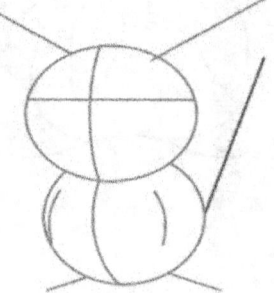

Step 3

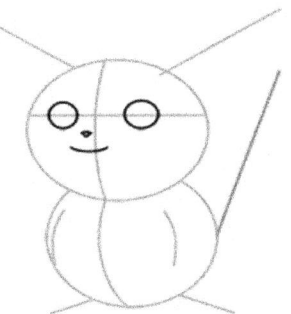

Step 4

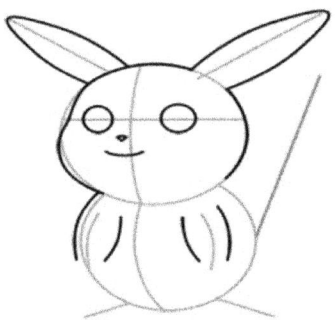

Step 5

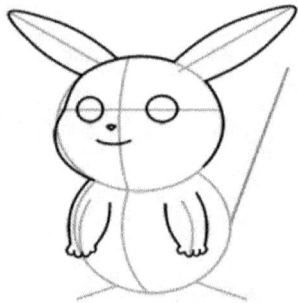

Step 6

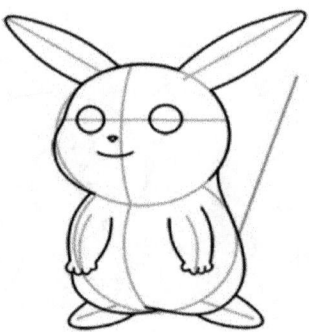

Step 7

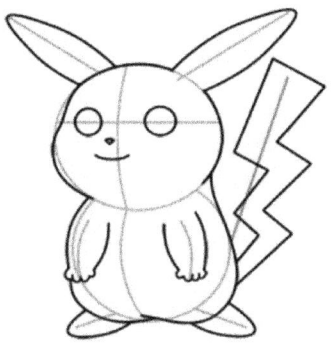

Step 8

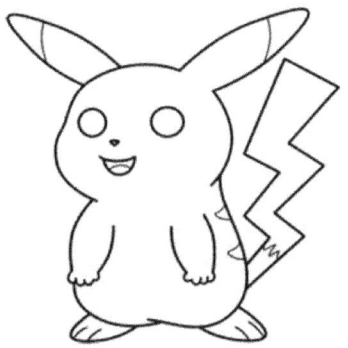